GUILTY AS CHARGED

A collection of short stories based on Landmark Judgements in the Indian Judiciary System

KRITHIKA MANI

Contents

Case 1
The Blueprint of Bio-Terrorism

Ataraxia, once vibrant and full of life, is now a chilling shadow of its former self. Five brutal years have passed since the bubonic plague, a twisted "gift" from a neighboring ally, ravaged the land. This deadly disease, carried by a swarm of test fleas, wove a web of despair across the nation. Science, the supposed savior, offered only flickers of hope amidst the relentless storm of death..

Then, a different spark ignited the ashes. Aidan, the enigmatic stepson of the fallen General Kieran, succumbed to the very plague he likely sought to conquer. But amidst this tragedy, a chilling truth emerged: it was murder, not the disease, that claimed him. The scene was a macabre tableau, meticulously staged, with one glaring omission - the identity of the killer.

Ihave never liked the color orange. In fact, simplifying my hatred for the same in a single sentence is a painful understatement. Take the orange paperback novel staring at me from across my now-packed desk. Each day I have to suppress the urge to toss it across the room and smack it at a ridiculous portrait of myself from not so long ago. It's safe to say this hatred started only seven months ago – the time when my father decided to bring home Ilsa, his fiancé! There it was, artfully plastered alongside the disgust on my face as my father's current beloved walked in.

Her tangerine gown seemed to suck the very color off our foyers' walls. My scrunched eyebrows seemed to become one as I glanced at the ribbons tying her creaking corset together. It made her dress resemble a painfully orange version of the tarantulas they kept at Scitraxia. The 9 year old rat like boy clutching her bejewelled arm did nothing to ease the arguably grotesque expression off of my face. The hatred most certainly did not disappear when the creature let out a squeal of delight as his undoubtedly sticky arms grabbed one of the action figures I had left on one of the chairs.

A quick sweep of the current predicament I was dragged into made it clear that my father, the General of Ataraxia, had finally found the woman he was going to make his seventh wife. As concerning as this might seem, Ataraxian culture had normalized having multiple short-lived marriages. In fact, the same was a symbol of power - and we all knew my father had to be the most powerful. But some other part of me couldn't help but feel rather suffocated. Something seemed different with the she-demon that Ilsa was. It seemed as though the aftermath from father's latest relationship was going to be much harder to move on from. Each warning light flashing in my mind drew me closer and closer to what made it all so different: my soon-to-be stepbrother, Aidan.

Whatever part of my conscience that my father hadn't stamped out attempted to argue with my sizzling hatred for the child. Was it right of me to hold so much negativity towards someone I have never even spoken to? What if, on some levels, Aidan could be the out I so desperately needed?

I was yanked from my thoughts with the familiar tapping noise of leather soles on expensive marble. The very lights seemed to shine brighter as my father strutted in, armor and all still on from the winter fete campaign shoot he had just finished. Flashing one of his signature smiles at Aidan, who had managed to make his way to a few feet ahead of me, sauntered on to embrace Ilsa.

"Is it done?" she crooned, as he stopped a few feet ahead of Aidan and me.

"The boys are now joint heirs to my empire." He said with a curt nod.

Those 9 words caused my entire future to crumble into nothing but little pieces of moondust, my eyes glazing with tears, utter rage and pent up disappointment. Ever since I was 9, my father had taken it upon himself to show me every nook and cranny of his estates, assets, and businesses, covering up the hours of my childhood taken away with the fact that someday, all of it was going to be mine. As much as I hated the long hours of work that were drilled into me at that delicate age, the one thing that had stuck with me was the fact that all of it was mine. If I had to choose between being a victim to the deadly plague engulfing our nations for years and cleaving my future into two, I would gladly choose to bear the consequences of the first. Never did I think that what was "mine" would ever have to become "ours".

But then it all fell into place. The "spontaneous" meetings my father had had with my governors this past month, the new wing he had installed parallel to mine, the uncanny amounts he quizzed me on company policies and proceedings. From that moment onwards I blocked out everything. The life around me went on - my father's rather painful justifications of his new administrator decision, my day-to-day conversations, Aidan's failed attempts at establishing some sort of friendship with me, and any other interaction I could. It seemed as though denial had become my only foe.

As overdramatic as it might seem, the few years went by with me continuing to reside in this state. All throughout the plague, even as I received numerous accolades and degrees, the times during which I brought 'Kieran and Co.' unattainable amounts of success - that feeling of impending doom never managed to leave me. It didn't help that my father attempted to throw Aidan and I together every chance he got, be it for mandatory rounds of the country, our classes, or his ridiculous mentor-mentee program. On some levels, I had to respect the effort he was putting into this but in my head the only thought that resided was the fact that it should all have been mine.

And then, without a second glance, he died. The great General of Ataraxia met his fate doing what he loved the most: soaring high above the stratosphere. One second he was here, the next second he was hurtling towards the ground, no control over his craft. Even in death he remained one of the biggest names in Ataraxian history, and I suppose that was the way he always wanted it. The lawyers came and went, and the only thing they seemed to repeat was the fact that both Aidan and I would share our fathers' assets.

Hours after the reading of my fathers will, I made my way across the city to the house of the one person I trust: Tate Fallon, my slightly psychotic, arguably radical, utterly genius best friend. I knew what I had to do, but I was as good as dead if I ever attempted it without him. It seemed as though the only solution to remove Aidan from my life was to use the one thing powerful enough to hold the entirety of Ataraxia down for years at an end: the plague.

Our plan was set into motion!

Tate was to take up a research position in the hi-tech laboratory in Sci-Traxia ,scale up the research ranks to make a request for samples containing the plague culture for "laboratory tests" - which wouldn't be out-of-the-blue. Due to the highly contagious nature of the plague cultures, his request would obviously be declined but the bigger picture would have been put into motion. Now that all the big names would know that Tate's request for the cultures, the next few aspects of our plan would come off as nothing out of the ordinary. Tate would then approach Dr Ukyl, a renowned scientist with a private state-of-the-art lab in the remote part of Ataraxia, stating that he had found a cure to the bubonic plague and would like to continue his research.

Purloining few samples of the deadly plague strains from Sci- Traxia, Tate joined Dr Ukyl's lab to produce a vial of the high concentration virus capable of working rapidly whilst I went out of my way to discreetly purchase large quantities of animals for us to test the cultures' effects upon.

Heady with the success of the project, armed with the lethal vial, Tate made his exit from the institute as hasty as possible and convinced the world's topmost researchers that he had to leave right in the midst of his experimentation due to a family member's health. He never went back. That's what made Tate and I so similar, we never looked back, we never made mistakes, and we always trusted that the other knew what he was doing. Up until then, we never thought there could be consequences - if only we knew.

On the 26th of November Aidan was set to go to college. A hopeful and bright 16 year old making his way into the world "an empire already on his shoulders", as my family so touchingly put it. He would take the bullet train to his dormitories and then come back to the estate by sundown for his farewell. The crowd was always large at the Ataraxian stations, and so a little brush of a shoulder or a prick on your arm is nothing of concern –until a dot of blood was seen on the arm of the heir!

But, as usual, my family couldn't seem to stand even one tiny dot on their star child's shoulder being out of place, The matter was soon brought to the attention of the doctors to the point where I had to intervene and use some borderline ancient "Our blood is the blood of warriors, what do you think father would say?" jargon in an attempt to stop the lab coat clad tiny man from taking a blood sample . I won't ever forget the look my Aunt Zahra gave as I completed what, at the time, I thought was a convincing monologue. She was always thought of as the sharpest and the coldest, but I guess some of us just disguise it better.

The fever struck Aidan like wildfire. By the time Aidan's letter informing us of the same reached our doorstep, he had become violently ill and his arm had become almost as thick as my skull. With my recommendations, Tate entered the royal chamber as Aidan's doctor, doing the family's medical bidding at beck and call, and managed to win over our family members and in the process gave Aidan doses of placebos to quell his sickness. Ilsa was stricken beyond herself, and I had to admit that I felt a shred of pity for her in those rare moments I passed by her wing, her sobs filling the air.

Aidan Kieran died five days later in the middle of the night. It had all worked out.

The same stuffed shirt white collar lawyers came along, documents in hand, foreheads scrunched and expressions neutral. It had all worked out - or so I thought. Looking back now, I see that my mistake lay in the fact that my constant state of denial and separation from those around me allowed me to miscalculate just how much those connected to us by blood needed answers, just how much they cared. It was in that moment that I realized that even though Aidan was gone, this was far from over. This game of chess now became something eerily similar to a conspiracy, a quest, and a war.

At the funeral, it took every ounce of my will to hold my aunt's icy gaze, penetrating my soul from meters away. My cousins and their parents stood huddled in a corner, some masking expressionless faces whilst others let out wails and sobs. Cameras flashed from every corner, reporters pushed up against the soundproofed glass doors separating our blood from all those who thrived as it fuelled their communities. With each step I took towards the podium to speak about Aidan with as much love and care I could muster; I could feel myself falling deeper and deeper into the rabbit hole.

In the corner of my eye, I could see a small man hobble past the barriers, the sounds of his canvas-clad feet and borderline tattered lab coat tearing into the silence that loomed behind him as he made his way towards Aunt Zahra.

"Ms. Kieran, Ms. Kieran!" he called, doing nothing to apologize for his disruption. She turned around just as the doors burst open and the Deputy Police Commissioner ran in, guns blazing and orders bursting out. The panting doctor continued, "We have blood cultures! You were correct he was murd-"

"Arrest him!" The commissioner called out, and it took me more time than it should have to realize that his cane was pointed at me. It's safe to say that the day had taken a turn. Gasps flew from all around as the officers the commissioner brought along cuffed me and plucked Tate out of the audience to do the same to him.

The next few weeks were a whirlwind of nothingness. To summarize hours and hours of court and the ever-so-wholesome family arguments that left my ears ringing, it seems as though Zahra, Isla and a few other members of my family didn't believe in the truth behind the circumstances of Aidan's death. They hired a team of investigators and went to the officials to incriminate whoever was responsible. They soon found the strains of plague in Aidan's system and connected it back to Tate's sudden requests for the cultures, found the receipts for the test animals and connected it back to the division of father's estates.

I now stand at my bleak office, gathering the last of my belongings and recounting these painful years while attempting to convince myself that I will not break. A gust of wind flies through the window and I hear the faint noise of paper rustling. Stuck towards the bottom of my portrait lay a hastily scrawled, half crumpled note. "Looks like 27 years worth of choosing to survive instead of thrive is ending in 24 hours" it said, in painfully orange ink. I chuckled as I tore the notes into bits, the ink piercing my vision in a manner that made it seem as though the paper itself was sneering at me.

Well, that was it. Life's grand slap in the face. It seems as though the one thing that stood beside me through all of this was neither a person nor was it money, it was hatred. Hatred for a color, and hatred for a brother. Poetic, isn't it?

The actual case in the Indian judiciary system

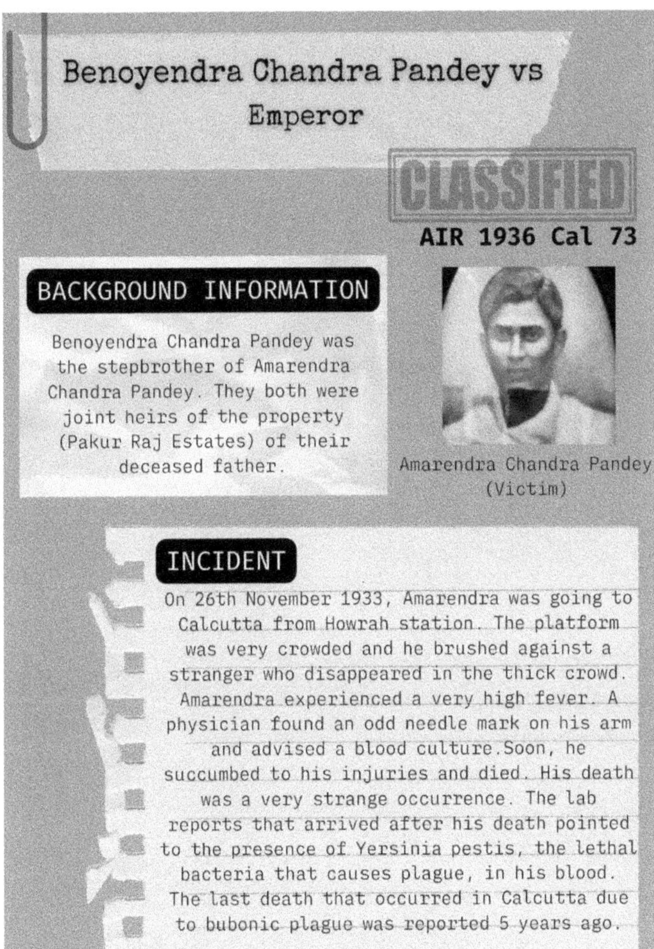

Benoyendra Chandra Pandey vs Emperor

CLASSIFIED

AIR 1936 Cal 73

BACKGROUND INFORMATION

Benoyendra Chandra Pandey was the stepbrother of Amarendra Chandra Pandey. They both were joint heirs of the property (Pakur Raj Estates) of their deceased father.

Amarendra Chandra Pandey
(Victim)

INCIDENT

On 26th November 1933, Amarendra was going to Calcutta from Howrah station. The platform was very crowded and he brushed against a stranger who disappeared in the thick crowd. Amarendra experienced a very high fever. A physician found an odd needle mark on his arm and advised a blood culture. Soon, he succumbed to his injuries and died. His death was a very strange occurrence. The lab reports that arrived after his death pointed to the presence of Yersinia pestis, the lethal bacteria that causes plague, in his blood. The last death that occurred in Calcutta due to bubonic plague was reported 5 years ago.

INVESTIGATION

- Contact Relatives
- Brief Chief
- Crime Scene Visit

Investigations by the Kolkata police unveiled a tangled web of conspiracy and a stubbornly audacious plot, involving purloining deadly bacteria from a hospital in Mumbai. On 16th February 1934, Benoyendra & his friend Taranath were arrested in the murder of one of Pakur Raj's heirs.

IN THE COURTROOM

The defence argued that Amarendra had been bitten by a rat flea. The court said the evidence proved that the two men accused of his murder had "stolen plague bacilli" from the Mumbai hospital and that "they could be carried to Calcutta and kept alive till 26th November 1933.The High Court reached the conclusion that the two sentenced men, Benoyendra Chandra Pandey and Taranath had contrived to murder Amarendra Chandra Pandey with an employed professional killer who was injected the plague culture into Amarendra in the crowded Howrah junction. The two men were life sentenced and deported to the Andamans.

LANDMARK JUDGEMENT

The Benoyendra Chandra Pandey Vs Emperor 1936 was the first case in India to use medical evidence to decide a case. One of the most important areas for courts to rule on was the assertion of a cause of death (whether it was natural or not). The blood culture report showing the presence of the plague virus clearly indicated that death of Amarendra was due to bubonic plague at a time when it was not prevalent in Calcutta. It was probably one of the first cases of individual bio-terrorism in the history of the modern world!

Notes

Notes

Case 2
Tangled in a Triangle

Five years ago, the world erupted in a cacophony of outrage. Shots were fired, both literal and metaphorical. A series of egregious mistakes ensnared the world's attention. Media outlets spun narratives, conspiracy theories sprouted like weeds, and court rulings only fueled the frenzy. At the center of this storm was a naval commander whose weapon discharge left one man dead.

Amidst the global uproar, one silent figure stood shrouded in the aftermath - the son of the man who pulled the trigger. How did this tragedy, etched into the world's memory, scar the life of the one left behind?

The beep of the handheld tape recorder filled the sitting room, its rhythm steadier than my heartbeat. The birds chirped outside, their melodies well organized and routine. The light made its way in and out at hourly increments. That was the nice thing about all things natural: they all had their own patterns, each part of their life moved on like clockwork from start to finish. This structure and pattern was all they needed to ensure some stability, and each of these parts of nature felt complete and content.

Then we come to humans. We seem to want to bide our time in havoc and uncertainty - it's almost like a drug. And just like with all other addictions, the lows are always worse than the highs. I suppose that crimes were the perfect examples of that lack of control the human race was so eager to explore. Arson by showing just how in a flash everything can be lost, grand larceny by depicting just how much control materialism had upon us, cybercrime describing the power that came with nobody knowing who you were - and then there was murder! Murder and everything in its aftermath seemed to be the least structured thing to circle this planet, far away from any semblance of a pattern.

All of a sudden, a hand waved in my face, the once-rapid noise of the handheld tape recorder now dissolved into nothingness. Tipping my chair backwards, I scraped the back of the same on the freshly painted periwinkle walls of the foyer.

"Parker, I had asked you a question? How would you describe the role of murder in your life since that seems to be such a big part of what you want to market from this interview? After all, the public will want to know what one of the Nashs have to say after 5 years." a voice said, my eyes focusing on the lady in front of me, fashionably donning her pair of gold-rimmed glasses around her neck and holding a vigorously scribbled upon notepad.

Ms. Ira Hawthorne, "a writer destined to establish her own true crime fanbase via her online magazine" or so it said on the rather unprofessional segment of her in the tabloids. Frankly, if she hadn't walked up to me and introduced herself, I would've pegged her for a librarian - whether or not that is a good thing is up to one's own interpretation.

"The concept of murder is something that is naturally frowned upon and rightfully so, but I highly doubt it's a concept that has embedded itself into someone's life as much as it has intertwined itself in mine. It is omnipresent. It is the centre of attention of my conversations at school, it takes over and jumps into my dreams at night, it influences each and every single thought, it stamps on my wildest dreams and tears at even the most basic desires." I said, allowing my heartbeat to increase at a snail's pace, a direct contrast to the simmering rage embedded deep down inside me.

"Although I, of all people, am not one to stop a classic inner monologue, I do suppose the interview calls for some foundation to all that. Some background into this utterly insightful glance into the obviously philosophical maturity residing within the teenage mind." as she droned on.

"Describe the event to me, leave no detail out. The press has no shortage of your parents' versions of the events, as well as Ashtons family's perspective but it seems to be missing out on just how groundbreaking the concept of an innocent child facing firsthand consequences of an act that drastic is. But in order for this groundbreaking series of revelations to come to light, you have to start at the same place everyone else does: the beginning - or atleast where you think it all began." ending her monologue with a retort. Although contrary to all the other retorts I had received within conversations, hers wasn't masked with condescension or a fight for power, it was nothing if not straightforward. Some part of me felt like opening up to her already.

"Due to my father's position in the military, it was safe to say that we moved around far more than the average family. But, no matter how much we moved, our house remained the same: a 3 bedroom villa, large windows, even larger living space, and a stunning lack of balconies. Even if those houses never felt like home, that sense of familiarity was worth more than words can convey. But then came the demanding tasks of adjusting to a new educational environment, learning one's likes and dislikes in that area, and familiarizing oneself with the residents of whatever town we migrated to. As exhausting and unnecessary each of those tasks seemed, I would be a fool to deny the fact that I was grateful for the fact that these moves armed me with an arsenal of social weapons, the most lethal arguably being the ability to read and see through people's emotions, actions and intentions as though they were tattooed onto their faces - even at ten years old." I said, mentally preparing myself to dive straight into what Ira seemed to be looking for.

"Ah, interesting metaphor. You seem to be one of the first nouveau riche kids who's able to hold his own this well, narration wise, all at the age of fifteen. However, some part of me can't help but ask if there was ever a time during which you wished you could give that socially analytical superpower back, a time where it might have done its job too well?" She said,

"About the metaphors, it's almost as though they're a hidden language - it's far easier to communicate with them. I suppose that in their own way, they've got a pattern. As for the question you asked me, it was a painfully prickly afternoon, the heat so bad it gave me a headache severe enough for me to be excused home. I heard two voices coming from my parents' room, getting closer and closer whilst I attempted to find something to shrink into. Our neighbor and my father's brother-in-arms, Ashton, stepped into the pile of unpacked boxes that made up our foyer, my mother Sybil a few strides behind him, both looking rather dishevelled, flushed and well, guilty. In that moment, I would have gladly chosen to give up my "superpower" and so as to avoid the hours I spent dissecting each expression, each movement, each stare and each blink - although I suppose this was the least dramatic thing to occur in the weeks to follow." I sighed and suppressed a laugh as Ira visibly moved closer towards the edge of her chair.

"Our family had met Ashton at numerous banquets, ceremonies and military events. I pegged him as a family guy, honest, faithful, worthy. Well, I suppose he was still a family man, just not to his own. After I saw Ashton and my mother, I re-entered the house this time announcing my entrance loud and clear, and just in perfect time for Ashton to form his own mutant personality of every nonchalant character he'd seen on television to convince himself that using the "I had to borrow some milk" excuse was obviously the most appropriate. However, some part of me did ache to believe him, and give or take a few seconds to my original entrance, and I probably would have." I ended with a sigh.

"What about the rest of your family? At the time how did you think they would fit into the scenario?" Ira asked, still steadily scribbling away on her notepad, blue ink tearing across the page in a frenzy.

"Well, Tahseen, my sister, would probably not have understood the depth of the issue, and she would've been more confused than anything because she was what, seven years old when it happened. As for my father, he happened to be away on duty for a while. However, even at the time I knew that his reaction was something only he could predict and fully comprehend. But I suppose it would be a crack in that calm-before-the-storm demeanor he always seems to have, and now we would finally get to see what happens after the calm passes. The week that my father returned made my household go from just that to a volcano waiting to erupt, except to everyone else, the volcano seemed to be a harmless flower. Bickering happened to be a primary mode of communication in my household. But suddenly, every small word muttered under one's breath, every single roll of one's eye, each snide comment, all had a painful amount of weightage. But of course, it never played out the way it was supposed to."

"We were all sitting eating a simple, early lunch, perfectly normal in the Nash household. It all went downhill in a flash: One second my father putting his arm around my mother as she flinched almost unnoticeably, the next he stormed off and she rushing off to the bedroom. I, on the other hand, had still not finished chewing a piece of my suddenly too cold cucumber sandwich."

"Was that all it took? Or could it have been the last straw?" Ira asked, the beads on the chain fastening her glasses to her neck twinkling in the same manner as her eyes.

I paused for a moment, visibly stunned by the path her inquisitiveness took her on this time. "I suppose in hindsight this could have been the last thing he was able to put up with. My parents barely spoke those weeks, but I never noticed because well, neither did I."

"Well, I suppose we should call it a day for today. I mean, what happened after Kenji found out Sybil was cheating on him isn't necessarily a secret." Ira said with a chuckle that could've directed to herself as much as it could've been to me.

To say that the rest of the story wasn't a secret might have been the biggest understatement of all time. Everything from the shirt my father wore as he dropped us off at the theatre mere hours later, the length of the interaction between Ashton's butler and my father, onto the number of rounds in the gun he shot Ashton with twice, and the exact conversation he had with the staff as he lied about his reason to "borrow" the gun from the locker he spontaneously saw as he picked up Ace, our dogs' medicine and the exact payphone he used to surrender himself were broadcasted on every news station, paper and form of communication that one could imagine. To this day every time someone walks past our now well-abandoned and half-destroyed house, the story of "the Nash case" grows wider and wider.

I packed up my things shortly after Ira left with promises to share the transcript of our conversation with me, happy for the day to be over. The bright and hopeful aura that existed prior to the beginning of this meeting slowly turned sour as I walked out of the building, earning a series of collective stares, whispers and not so subtle pointing. From our childhood, we learnt that curiosity killed the cat. Someday, people will realize that all that happened in this case was that it went above and beyond to kill each animal in the farm and leave half the farm broken in its wake. After all, who would know better than I do? Who knows, maybe even murder has some pattern to it.

The actual case in the Indian judiciary system

K M Nanavati vs State of Maharastra

CLASSIFIED

BACKGROUND INFORMATION

K M Nanavati, who is the accused in the present case, was appointed as the second officer in command of INS Mysore. In 1949, he married Sylvia and eventually moved to Bombay with his family. The husband and wife became friends with a businessman , Prem Ahuja who later began to have an extra-marital relationship with Sylvia.

AIR 1962 SC 605

KM Nanavati
(Accused)

INCIDENT

On the afternoon on April 27, 1959, Nanavati discovered his wife's affair with Ahuja. Later in the day, dropped his wife and children at a cinema hall, picked up his pistol from his boat and reached Ahuja's flat.

The confrontation with Prem Ahuja took a violent turn as Nanavati ended firing two unintentional shot which ended up killing the victim. After this, Nanavati drove himself to the police station and surrendered himself to the authorities.

INVESTIGATION

The slugs that killed Ahuja came from the pistol that was in the possession of the accused. Nanavati's narration of the fight with Ahuja in the restroom did not prove to be fully true and with noimportant specifics. The wounds found on the body of the victim did not seem unintentional, but to the contrary, seemed very predictable in a case where the shooter is in close range with the victim. Different conditions brought out in the proof additionally build-up that there couldn't have been any fight between Nanavati and Ahuja. The investigation showed that the shooting was conscious and intentional and not to the contrary.

IN THE COURTROOM

K.M. Nanavati, the accused, initially was declared not guilty under Section 302 by the Jury with an 8 : 1 verdict. The case was then referred by the Sessions Judge to the Hon'ble High Court of Bombay under Section 307 of the Code of Criminal Procedure, 1973. The Court in this case held that the murder was a well-processed and thoughtful one, which certainly did not attract Exception 1 of Section 300 of the Indian Penal Code. Eventually, Nanavati was pardoned by the then Governor of Maharastra, Vijayalakshmi Pandit . He then migrated to Canada with his wife and children.

LANDMARK JUDGEMENT

A milestone case in criminal history of India, Nanavati case with its large media exposure has a legendary status in the Indian legal world. It was instrumental in abolishing Jury System in India and secondly, the Power of Pardon was taken away from the Governors of the State.

Contact Relatives

Brief Chief

Crime Scene Visit

Notes

Notes

Case 3

Suspended Amongst the Spirits

Ravania, a village pulsing with life despite its modest size, held a secret. Whispers of spectral inhabitants flitting through the abandoned fields and desolate streets were not new. But were these rumored ghosts benevolent or something more sinister? The line between folklore and reality blurred, and the question lingered.

Three unsuspecting men, oblivious to the village's whispered truth, found themselves entangled in its heart. One night, fate would rewrite the narrative, revealing the unsettling answer - friend, foe, or something else entirely?

"Ghosts." The word seemed to echo, as though bits and pieces of the memories from that night lay artfully splayed on the ebony walls itself.

"I'm sorry, could you repeat that?" Judge Nassar asked, his eyebrows now parallel with the wrinkles on his forehead.

"Ghosts, spirits, supernatural beings, demons, whatever fits the situation best." I spat out, each of the 'confidence tips' that Eris had given me left my mind as quickly as the breath I loosened before answering the Judge's rather pointed question.

The opposition lit up, as though their glee was embedded into their very skin cells. "Just to clarify, the respondent is stating that not only is he guilty of the crime he is being charged with, he is also justifying his actions by saying he thought he was attacking…. ghosts?" their lawyer whose name seemed to slip my mind said, his smirk hidden as well as the concerning amounts of gel he threw into his hair.

My lawyer, Eris Andras, shot up like an arrow. With a quick glance around the courtroom, it seemed as though the next words to leave his mouth would do nothing to support our case. Ever since we knew I was to be present at trial, it seems as though Eris had taken upon himself to recite a word-to-word reading of the letter from court every few minutes. But, as much as I complained, that letter ensured that I wouldn't be charged as guilty until I admitted it explicitly - courtesy of my "manic state and the compromised integrity coming with it". It seemed to be the only thing keeping me out of jail.

The air seemed to quieten when I stood up, cutting Eris off. Everyone and everything seemed to stop in anticipation - including the seemingly omnipresent quivering of my mustache. As the jury's pointed stares pierced my very will to live, I realized that I truly had not thought this out. But what harm could one more mistake do? How much worse could it possibly get? Well, it seemed as though I now had no choice but to find out.

"If it pleases the court, there is something I would like to say" I could almost hear the grimacing expressions staring at me from all corners of the courtroom. Beside me, Eris let out a sigh so sad it made one think he had just kissed his career goodbye.

"Before that, can we approach your Honor?" the opposition cut in, chairs already being dragged back, their lawyers ready to pounce. Judge gave a curt nod, his eyes swimming with curiosity, his fingers twirling around his mustache just as they did everytime he found something outright "damning" according to Eris' prior research. As the lawyers stood up, their formation mimicked the ones I had seen in the countless war-room preparations that the all-boys boarding school I went to forced us to sit through.

That's when I saw it: the uncanny and utterly unnecessary resemblance between the lawyers' flowy pitch-black cloaks and whatever it was I saw that night. It passed momentarily, as though I was being mocked while being forced into that lethal sense of calm that I had once succumbed to in fear. A tug that I hadn't felt in a while invaded my senses, my breath starting to quicken and my throat closing up.

I forced myself to think about anything else, anything at all. How the wooden chairs creaked in harmony whenever someone sat in the last row, the similarities between the flow of the coats and the flow of the ghosts, the way that the chandelier twinkled with every gust of the hot summer wind, the smell of the bodies in the wind after that night, the sound of the court reporter's broken typewriter and the way it changes with each key, the crack that filled the air as I hit the body, the resounding echo of the Judges gavel on the soundblock, the shivers that ran through me as I tore away from the crime scene, the clear yet muffled voices of the opposition, the red, warm, and sticky blood. The blood that cascaded off the walls and slid through the blades of grass, the blood that stained my hands and haunted me at every opportunity, the blood that ingrained itself into every waking moment of whatever life I had left.

"Please proceed Mr. Tamar. Remember, you are under oath." Judge Nassar said, his voice cutting straight through my daze and earning a small scoff from the opposition's side. I stood on visibly shaking legs, the once suppressible tug and mania now consuming me, controlling my every move.

"It's funny isn't it." I said, as I barked a laugh out in an attempt to ease the tightness that overtook my throat, "Those wigs they force you to wear? I feel like my grandmother's staring at me from above and beyond! Ah, we're back to ghosts, that's even funnier."

"Oh I know what it is! Those wigs look as though they were made out of the fur of those missing goats from last week, don't they Eris?" I said, squinting at the sheet-faced Eris, my eyes tearing against their sockets and my arms flailing around, "God, I still remember you prattling on and on about those damned goats, well, I think they're dead. Ha! Dead. Dead-dead-dead. Dead…Dead-dead. De- I could just go on and on!"

"Mr. Tamar." Judge Nassar warned, his voice struggling to maintain the professionalism the court so desperately needed. He stood up, his cloak flying back while his and the now standing opposition's chairs let out a cacophony of wails. And then I lost it - even more, that is.

A scream tore out of me, so toe-curling it sent the court reporter and her paper's flying against the wall. I fell to my knees, a jagged splinter of wood piercing into my dominant leg as I rammed my fists against the hard yet comforting floor in an attempt to break through it and flee.

"Security!" I heard Judge Nassar shriek, the word briefly cutting into my emphatic screams, yet coming from a place far, far away, barely registering in my brain. The guards rushed in, weapons drawn and smoulders blazing, and I let out a scream so otherworldly it seemed to drown out everything else. Judge Nassar stuttered, visibly shaken and at a loss for words - and I doubted I could blame him.

Observing this particular spectacle from third person would be nothing if not concerning. Eris rushed over to the bench and frantically whispered something in Nassar's ear, his hands dramatically flailing around.

"Everyone, we're now going to move to a short recess." Judge Nassar said as he shook his head, clearly still reeling from my rather traumatizing inner monologue. Hands eased me up into the air, and everything around me seemed to be dazed, as though my vision was yet to catch up with the rest of my senses. Somewhere to my right, I heard the familiar set of creaks and groans the courtrooms doors made each time they were opened, and a blinding light soon engulfed me. I felt the oddly comforting feeling of being placed on metal bench, and I smelt the familiar freshness of the courthouse lawns. A familiar sense of dread seemed to take over when the guards placed me onto the bench completely, but it flashed past in a blink as I took in Eris familiar sandalwood cologne entering the air near me. He didn't have to say anything for me to understand just how disappointed he was.

"Frankly, I can't believe that Judge Nassar didn't have you thrown into prison just for that outburst. You want to enlighten me on what went on in there or should I just go ahead and drop the case?" He said, his stoic demeanor somehow making its way into his voice as well. It seemed as though this was Eris' own version of the calm before the storm - yet this storm seemed as though it would be tailored to orchestrate nothing but my downfall.

"In order to do so I have to tell you about that night. All of it." I said, my voice trembling.

The very notion of explaining that unfathomable series of unfortunate events sent shivers down my spine. It was something I had tried my best to avoid doing throughout these long weeks because frankly, it terrified me. How could I possibly explain that night to someone else before I had even come to terms with it? On top of all of that, explaining the same in less than an hour? Utter blasphemy. I chuckled at the thought, earning a scorn from Eris, who sat beside me, leg shaking impatiently. With a sigh, I let myself sink into those memories, let myself be one with whatever overcame me that night, and let myself harmonize with the beliefs that were churned into my very childhood.

"What do you know about superstitions, Eris? Myths, magic, witchcraft and everything in between.

I suppose it might sound delusional, and frankly I'd be more surprised if it wasn't. To the citizens of the small town Ravania, however, it was anything but. Our town was one that prided itself upon its mythical knowledge and its strange sightings of all things surreal."

"Spreading the knowledge and the wary mindset that came with these beliefs was something that was prioritized at a level similar to the way most cities prioritized its education, health and economy. While other towns worked on expansion, infrastructure, and establishing secure means of trade, Ravania kept to itself, weaving more tales to broaden the aura of mystique that our land thrived upon. In hindsight the amount of time and energy that we put into, " I said, my breath catching as I let it all flow out.

"Our town came into existence 270 years ago, and it was originally a land so bleak there were painfully limited ways in and out. It started out small, and with time it was clear that it intended to remain that way. It was almost gatekept but done so in a manner that safeguarded its citizens and shielded them from harsh realities just enough."

"In the beginning these rumors had no power, they were protected within their own atmosphere of facts and fibs - they were protected, in a certain sense. Their existences came and went, brief moments on a larger timeline, making their way into household to household, from generation to generation. Stories of the ghosts of a former family member, the spirits promising power, love, money, the demons that 'possessed' children - you name it, someone in our town had a story about it. In theory, it seems nothing if not utopic, a necessary break from the bleakness of everything outside our nation, but at one point it was nothing if not ever consuming. As time went on, the rumors centered themselves to begin within or around the vicinity of the abandoned aerodrome towards the outskirts of our town. The area was so abandoned it might've never existed, and the additional precaution of a word-of-mouth "rule" warning all citizens against activity after dark was spread throughout the town. That night, the night where it all happened, the line between delusion and real-life was dangerously thin. What started out as nothing but a bet with no grounds to do any harm, ended up both changing and ending lives." I gasped as the thoughts flowed out like a swollen river.

"It started out as a gamble between my landlord, Kent, my boss, Jafar, and I. I suppose, in hindsight, it does seem as though the unnatural nature of the trio seemed to have foreshadowed the events to follow. We believed the terms of our bet would be inconsequential and ordinary: at the stroke of midnight, whoever got closest to the aerodrome would well be crowned the winner - nothing more nothing less. It all seemed so superficial at the time, purely egoistic and fuelled by a series of arguably irrelevant decisions, the usual lack of control, words uttered without thought, and meaningless threats. As we made our way past Ravania's signature stilt houses, each one already locked and bolted even though the night was still young, I suppose each one of us had our own reservations about the magnitude of the actual bet. But the power that came with winning the bet and the insatiable hunger for the same was far more in-control than whatever part of rationality that remained." I shuddered, pausing to catch both my breath and my thoughts, both of which were going faster than handleable. As much as he would have loved to disagree, there was no denying that Eris sat on the very edge of his seat as I droned on and on.

"While we paced around in our heads contemplating just how good of an idea the bet was, we seemed to have reached the aerodrome. We stood there for mere seconds before something went wrong. All of a sudden, a series of lights flickered and disappeared just as quickly, in perfect sync with the seemingly humanesque howling of the wind. In the three minutes that we all stood rooted to our spots, every senses paused in utter shock, the lights seemed to get closer and closer, the howling rapidly increasing in volume, and black figures began spinning all around. Before I knew it, I was engulfed in a state of apparent clarity and calm, swinging the socially required knife I carried in all directions, unaware of the damage I was doing. I could have been trapped in that daze for seconds, hours, or minutes and neither would I have known nor would I have stopped. All I remember after this point were brief flashes: a rush of guilt as I stare at my bloodstained hands and shirt, insane amounts of anxiety whilst I stared at three utterly destroyed bodies not knowing which would live to see the morning, Jafar and Kent's muffled voices trying to bring me back from this unnatural state, the blinding lights of the nearby hospital, and the cold metal of handcuffs biting into my skin."

"For a while I didn't even know who I had hurt, what I had done to them, and what would happen after. All that I saw was the blank wall in my cell and the blank state of my mind, as though I was frozen in time. I remember them now, Eris, they were the three Miles sisters, just attempting to gather some flowers that sprouted in the area around the aerodrome for a religious ceremony. I attacked one, Eris. All because of what I thought was a ghost. It seems as though one can never know what gamble could turn into the final gambit." And then I shattered inside, desperately gulping down mouthfuls of air.

Eris walked away, muttering to himself about bail, polling the jury and sidebar,

the words almost floating around him like some sort of animated character. He stopped in his tracks, now a few meters away and turned.

"Ghosts?" He let out, layers of uncertainty not bothering to hide themselves.

"The only reason I did what I did."

He motioned for me to join him and we walked back in, a little more ready to face the rest of the world. It all seemed so simple, albeit painfully so. Turns out that in the end, the most terrifying ghosts aren't those of supernatural origin, nor those that blossom in both fear and triumph. In reality, the ghosts that leave the most in their wake are those that dwell within the consequences of our actions. The ones that thrive on the damage that your decisions leave behind.

The actual case in the Indian judiciary system

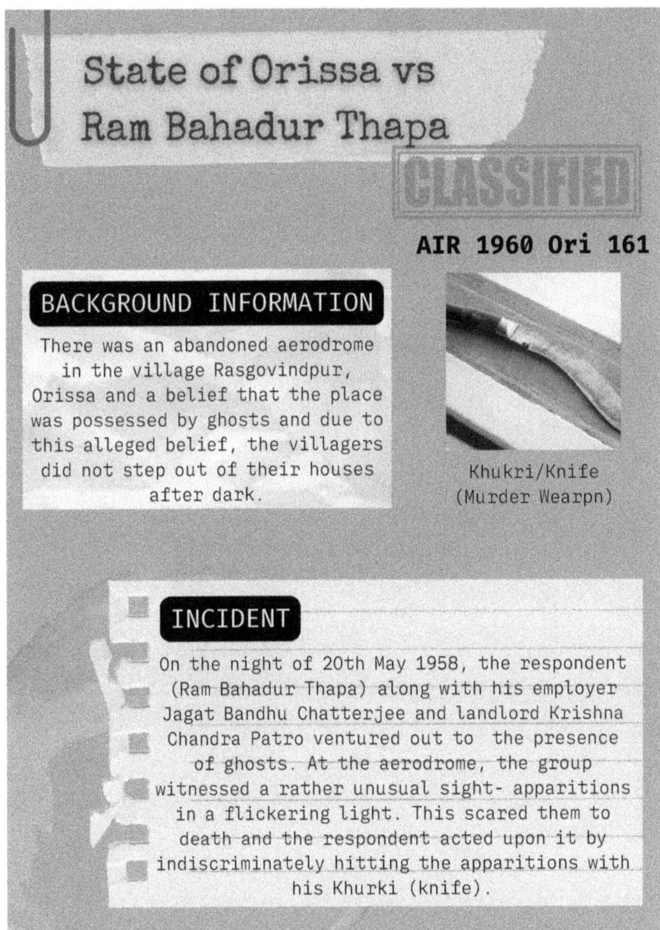

Contact Relatives

Brief Chief

Crime Scene Visit

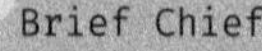

INVESTIGATION

The apparent ghosts in the flickering light were a group of women from a nearby village. These women had come to gather 'Mohua' flowers at night. Ram Bahadur Thapa's attack took the life of Gelhi Majhiani, and grievously injured two other women. For this heinous act, Ram Bahadur Thapa was charged for murder.

IN THE COURTROOM

The counsel for the respondent, Ram Bahadur Thapa contented that the respondent had neither the necessary criminal intention or knowledge for his act and when he attacked the victims. He believed that he was attacking ghosts and not human beings.

The judge acquitted Mr. Thapa and based his decision on the reasoning of bona fide mistake of fact, which comes under Section 79 of the IPC.

LANDMARK JUDGEMENT

The benefit of section 79 of IPC is provided to a person who by reason of mistake of fact in good faith and believes himself to be justified by law in doing an act. With the circumstance in this case, it was clear that the respondent believed that he was attacking ghosts and hence he was entitled to get protection from section 79 of IPC. The duty of the law is to guarantee that the defense of mistake of facts isn't abused or justice isn't denied to the victims.

Notes

Notes

Case 4

Shadows of Justice

The town of Velora was a place of shadows, where the lines between right and wrong were often obscured by the dark clouds that hung low in the sky. In the heart of this otherworldly town, a quiet struggle for justice was brewing, sparked by a tragedy that would forever alter its course. When Amara, a social worker with a heart as vast as the deserts surrounding Velora, stood up against the old customs that chained her town to its past, she had no idea of the storm she would unleash.

As Amara fought to protect the vulnerable, she herself became a target. What followed was a story of resilience, a battle against the invisible forces that sought to keep her silent. In the town's dim alleys and forgotten corners, a group of women gathered under the banner of justice, determined to reshape their world. But in a place where justice itself could be a shadow, the question remained: would they emerge victorious, or would they too be consumed by the darkness that loomed over Velora?

In the bleak, wind-swept plains of Velora, a town that seemed perpetually shrouded in a gray mist, Amara Devine stood out as a glimmer of hope. A dedicated social worker, Amara's life was a constant battle against the suffocating traditions that held her community in an iron grip. Her latest mission was her most perilous yet— preventing the sacrificial rite of a young girl, a custom that had been practiced in Velora for centuries.

Despite the ominous warnings from the town's elders and the oppressive atmosphere that seemed to hang over her like a dark cloud, Amara pressed on. She knew the risks she was taking, but the thought of that innocent child's fate fuelled her determination. However, she also knew that her defiance of the old ways would not go unpunished.

One evening, as the last vestiges of a dying sun struggled to pierce through the thick, toxic haze, Amara's world was torn apart. A group of men, chosen enforcers of Velora's ancient traditions, cornered her in an abandoned alley. The assault that followed was not just an act of physical brutality—it was a vicious attempt to break her spirit, to remind her and every other woman in Velora that they were powerless against the town's dark customs.

The news of Amara's attack spread rapidly through Velora's narrow, labyrinthine streets, igniting a spark of outrage in a town long resigned to its fate. But at the heart of the chaos was a woman who refused to be silenced. Amara's fight for justice became a rallying cry, a symbol of resistance against a system that had failed its people for too long. But she knew that her quest for justice would be met with indifference, if not outright hostility, in a place where silence had become a way of life.

In the distant, towering spires of the High Tribunal of Novark, a group of women's rights defenders gathered, their faces set with determination. They called themselves Velka, a name derived from the ancient word for victory. United by their shared anger and a fierce resolve, they vowed to take up Amara Devine's cause, not just for her, but for all the women of Velora who had suffered in silence for generations.

The women of Velka knew that this was not merely a case—it was a catalyst for change, an opportunity to challenge the very core of Veloran society. Under their banner, they filed a petition in the High Tribunal of Novark, arguing that the absence of any protective measures against sexual violence violated the fundamental rights of women, rights that were supposed to be guaranteed by the Covenant of the Free States.

Their petition was more than a legal document—it was a desperate plea for justice, an urgent call for the Tribunal to recognize the widespread issue of sexual violence in Velora and the void of any legal framework to combat it. The courtroom soon became the battleground where Velka's warriors, armed with truth and righteousness, fought for the rights of women who had been denied justice for far too long.

The atmosphere in the High Tribunal was thick with tension as the case of Velka vs. The Dominion of Velora began. The Tribunal's chamber, with its high, vaulted ceilings and eerie, blue-hued lighting, was filled with advocates, spectators, and the curious alike. All eyes were on the proceedings, for this case had the potential to change the very fabric of the Veloran society.

Velka's legal team, led by the formidable advocate Sorcha Vance, presented their arguments with precision and an unwavering resolve. Sorcha spoke with the fire of someone who had spent her entire life fighting for the rights of the oppressed. She argued that the failure to protect women like Amara from violence and harassment was a gross violation of their fundamental rights, rights enshrined not only in the Covenant but also in the universal principles that governed all sentient beings.

As Sorcha's words reverberated through the chamber, a heavy silence fell. The justices of the Tribunal, their faces obscured by the soft, cerulean glow of the chamber, listened with rapt attention. They knew that the decisions they made in this case would ripple far beyond Velora, possibly setting a precedent for the entire Free States.

On the other side, the representatives of Velora's Dominion struggled to mount a defense. Their arguments, mired in outdated customs and half-hearted justifications, were weak at best. The justices, one by one, questioned them with a growing intensity, their dissatisfaction evident. It became clear that the old ways were on trial, and their time was running out.

In an unprecedented move, the High Tribunal acknowledged the severity of the case and the urgent need for action. The justices, realizing that the existing laws were woefully inadequate, decided to take matters into their own hands. They chose to craft a new set of directives, a temporary yet powerful legal framework until the legislators of the Free States could draft comprehensive laws.

Drawing upon the Covenants and international conventions, as well as the evolving norms of other Free States, the justices introduced what would come to be known as the Velka Edicts. These edicts were revolutionary, mandating that all employers and institutions in Velora take immediate and concrete steps to protect women from harassment and violence. This included the creation of oversight committees, mandatory awareness programs, and a clear process for filing and addressing complaints.

The Velka Edicts were more than just guidelines; they were a powerful message to the entire Free States. They declared that the time had come to confront the deeply rooted, oppressive practices that had long been excused in the name of tradition. The edicts sent shockwaves through Velora, shaking its rigid social structures to their core and forcing even the most conservative elements of society to acknowledge the need for change.

The announcement of the Velka Edicts was like a thunderclap across the murky skies of Velora. For the first time in living memory, women had a legal instrument that they could wield to defend their rights. Institutions and employers across Velora were compelled to comply with the edicts, from the smallest artisanal guilds to the grand councils that governed the city-states.

The edicts also ignited a wider conversation about gender and power, something that had long been suppressed in Velora. Women who had once been too afraid to speak up began to share their stories, drawing strength from one another. The media, which had previously turned a blind eye to such issues, began to cover these stories, amplifying the voices of the voiceless and forcing the broader public to confront the uncomfortable truths that had been buried for so long.

But the impact of the Velka Edicts was not confined to Velora alone. Across the Free States, from the gleaming metropolises to the smallest outposts, people began to question their own practices and policies. The Edicts became a symbol of resistance and empowerment, showing that even in the most oppressive environments, change was possible when people had the courage to stand up for what was right.

Despite the triumph of the Velka Edicts, the fight for true justice was far from over. The implementation of the edicts across Velora faced numerous challenges. In some places, the response was lukewarm at best, with institutions creating committees on paper but doing little to address the underlying issues. Elsewhere, the old power structures resisted change, using every tactic at their disposal to undermine the new directives.

Amara Devine's personal quest for justice was a stark reminder of the long road ahead. While the Velka Edicts had brought her some measure of solace, her attackers remained at large, protected by the same corrupt systems that had failed her in the first place. The courts in Velora, mired in bureaucratic delays and outdated procedures, acquitted the men who had brutalized her, citing lack of evidence and the unreliability of witnesses.

The verdict was a bitter blow to Amara and her supporters, a harsh reminder that while laws could change, deep-seated societal attitudes were much harder to shift. But Amara refused to give in to despair. She knew that her fight was part of a much larger struggle, one that would continue long after her story was told.

The Velka case sparked a movement that spread like wildfire across the Free States. Women's rights groups, civil society organizations, and even some progressive elements within the government began to rally around the cause. The movement called for the full implementation of the Velka Edicts and pushed for the creation of a comprehensive legal framework to protect women from harassment and violence.

As the movement gained momentum, it became clear that the Velka Edicts were just the beginning. The people demanded more than temporary guidelines—they wanted a permanent, robust legal system that would ensure the safety and dignity of all women in the Free States.

In response to this groundswell of public support, the legislative bodies of the Free States began drafting what would eventually become the Law for the Protection of Women in Public and Private Spaces. This law, passed in the wake of the Velka case, was a comprehensive and far-reaching piece of legislation that built upon the foundation laid by the Velka Edicts.

Today, the Velka case is remembered as a watershed moment in the history of the Free States. It was a case that not only brought justice to Amara

Devine but also changed the lives of millions of women across the realms. The Velka Edicts, and the subsequent laws that followed, are now entrenched in the legal frameworks of the Free States, serving as a beacon of hope for those who continue to fight for equality and justice. The legacy of Velka lives on in the many women who now walk the streets of Velora and beyond with their heads held high, no longer shackled by the fear of the past.

But with change came resistance. The deeply entrenched power structures in Velora, those who had long benefited from the oppression and subjugation of women, did not take kindly to their newfound power being challenged. Secret gatherings were held in the dark corners of the city, where whispers of rebellion against the new laws grew louder. The old guard, composed of influential figures from the ancient families of Velora, conspired to undermine the movement. They spread propaganda, twisting the narrative to paint the Velka Edicts as an attack on Veloran traditions and values.

Amara Devine, who had become a symbol of the fight against oppression, was frequently targeted. Her every move was scrutinized, and attempts were made to discredit her, to paint her as an outsider, an enemy of Velora's "heritage." Yet, Amara remained unbowed. She knew that the journey towards justice was fraught with challenges, and she was prepared to face them head-on.

Sorcha Vance, Velka's lead advocate, continued to lead the legal battle, often finding herself at odds with powerful adversaries who sought to weaken the Velka Edicts. But Sorcha, with her unyielding resolve and sharp legal mind, stood firm. She knew that the Edicts were more than just a set of rules—they were a promise to the women of Velora that they would no longer have to suffer in silence.

Despite the opposition, the movement continued to grow. More women, and even some men, joined the cause, realizing that the fight for women's rights was a fight for the soul of Velora. Educational programs were established, teaching the youth about the importance of gender equality and respect for all individuals. The media played a crucial role, continuing to expose cases of injustice and rallying public support for the implementation of the Velka Edicts.

The ripple effects of the movement were felt far and wide. Neighboring city-states began adopting similar measures, inspired by the courage and resilience of the women of Velora. International organizations took notice, offering support and resources to strengthen the movement. The once-isolated town of Velora had become a symbol of hope and change, a beacon of what could be achieved when people stood together against injustice.

In the streets of Velora, once filled with fear and oppression, there was now a palpable sense of hope. Women walked freely, their spirits no longer crushed by the weight of centuries-old traditions. The Velka Edicts had done more than just provide legal protection—they had ignited a cultural shift, one that was slowly but surely dismantling the patriarchal structures that had long governed Veloran society.

Years passed, and the town of Velora transformed. The once-dark and foreboding streets were now alive with color and life. New institutions were established, focusing on the empowerment of women and marginalized communities. The schools, once bastions of traditionalist thought, became places where young minds were nurtured in the principles of equality, justice, and respect for all.

Amara Devine, though older and scarred by her experiences, remained a guiding force in the community. She became a mentor to the next generation of activists, sharing her story and the lessons she had learned in her fight for justice. Her name was synonymous with strength and resilience, a symbol of the power of the human spirit to overcome even the most daunting of challenges.

Sorcha Vance, too, continued her work, now as a senior figure in the legal reforms that were being instituted across the Free States. The laws that had been inspired by the Velka Edicts were continuously refined and expanded, ensuring that no woman, in Velora or elsewhere, would ever have to suffer in silence again.

The young women of Velora, who had grown up in the shadow of these monumental changes, were determined to carry the torch forward. They organized, they advocated, and they led with a vision of a society that was truly just and equitable. The movement that had started with a plea for justice in a small, oppressed town had blossomed into a global force for change.

As Velora and the broader Free States moved towards a future of greater equality, the story of the Velka case became a legend, passed down through generations. It was taught in schools, studied by scholars, and celebrated in the arts. The names of

Amara Devine, Sorcha Vance, and the women of Velka were etched into the annals of history, their legacy a testament to the power of collective action and the unyielding pursuit of justice.

In time, Velora became known not just for its dark past, but for its remarkable transformation. It became a model for other regions, demonstrating that even the most deeply rooted traditions of oppression could be challenged and overcome. The world watched as Velora's journey from a town of despair to a beacon of hope inspired similar movements in distant lands.

The landscape of Velora itself began to change. The oppressive gray mist that had once enveloped the town seemed to dissipate, replaced by a clearer, brighter atmosphere. It was as if the town itself was shedding its old skin, emerging renewed and revitalized, ready to embrace the future.

In the twilight of her life, Amara Devine often found herself reflecting on the journey she had been a part of. She would walk through the streets of Velora, seeing the bustling markets, the vibrant murals that adorned the walls, and the joyful faces of young women who now had the freedom to dream, to aspire, and to achieve.

Amara knew that the fight for justice was never truly over—that there would always be new challenges to face, new battles to fight. But she also knew that what they had achieved in Velora was something extraordinary. They had proven that even in the darkest of places, change was possible when people stood together, united in their belief in a better world.

Sorcha Vance, still as sharp as ever, continued to push for reforms, ensuring that the momentum they had built was not lost. She knew that the legal frameworks they had established were just the beginning and that the real work lay in changing hearts and minds. But she was confident that the foundation they had laid would endure, providing a strong base for future generations to build upon.

As the sun set over Velora, casting a golden hue over the town, it was clear that the journey was far from over. The movement that had started with the Velka case had spread beyond the borders of Velora, touching lives in ways that its founders could never have imagined.

In the far reaches of the Free States, in towns and cities where the old ways still held sway, there were new Amaras and Sorchas, ready to take up the mantle. They were inspired by the story of Velora, by the courage of those who had come before them, and by the belief that a better world was possible.

The struggle for justice, for equality, and for the dignity of all individuals would continue. But Velora's story had shown the world that no matter how deep the darkness, there was always the possibility of light. And that light, once kindled, could spread, illuminating even the darkest corners of the earth.

Years turned into decades, and the story of Velora became legend. The Velka Edicts were enshrined in the legal systems of the Free States, serving as a model for similar laws across the world. Amara Devine and Sorcha Vance became icons, their names synonymous with the fight for justice and equality.

But perhaps the greatest legacy of the Velka case was the realization that change was not just possible—it was inevitable, as long as people were willing to stand up and demand it. Velora had transformed from a town of fear and oppression into a symbol of hope and resilience, proving that the power to change the world lies within each of us.

In the end, the story of Velora is not just the story of one town or one movement. It is the story of all of us—the story of the human spirit's unyielding quest for justice, for equality, and for a world where everyone, regardless of their gender, their background, or their circumstances, can live with dignity and respect. And that story, as it continues to unfold, will forever be shaped by the echoes of justice that began in Velora.

The actual case in the Indian judiciary system

Vishaka and Others vs State of Rajasthan

BACKGROUND INFORMATION

AIR 1997 SC 3011

This case was brought before the Supreme Court of India by a group of women's rights activists following the brutal gang rape of Bhanwari Devi, a social worker in Rajasthan who was targeted for trying to stop child marriage. The activists, under the banner of the organization Vishaka, filed a public interest litigation (PIL) seeking justice for Bhanwari Devi and protection for women in workplaces.

Bhanwari Devi
(The woman behind Vishaka Guidelines)

INCIDENT

The petitioners argued that the lack of effective legal redress for sexual harassment at the workplace violated women's fundamental rights to gender equality, life, and liberty as enshrined in the Constitution of India. The case highlighted the pervasive issue of sexual harassment and the absence of specific legal provisions to address it.

IN THE COURTROOM

The Supreme Court, recognizing the severity of the issue, decided to establish guidelines to fill the legislative void. The court examined international conventions and norms to formulate these guidelines, emphasizing the need for immediate measures to protect working women from sexual harassment.

LANDMARK JUDGEMENT

The Supreme Court delivered a landmark judgment by establishing the "Vishaka Guidelines" for the prevention of sexual harassment at the workplace. These guidelines mandated employers to take specific steps to prevent and address complaints of sexual harassment. The judgment significantly contributed to creating safer work environments for women across India and led to the eventual enactment of the Sexual Harassment of Women at Workplace (Prevention, Prohibition and Redressal) Act, 2013.

IMPORTANCE

This case is important because it established a legal framework for addressing sexual harassment in the workplace, ensuring the protection of women's rights to equality and dignity. The Vishaka Guidelines laid the groundwork for future legislation and brought national attention to the issue of workplace harassment.

Contact Relatives

Brief Chief

Crime Scene Visit

Notes

Notes

Case 5
The Cook's Tale

The sprawling mansion in New Delos was a world unto itself, filled with the smells of spices and the soft murmur of conversations that floated like whispers on the wind. It was here that Devraj, a humble cook, found himself amidst the unfolding of a tale that would shake the very foundations of his understanding of freedom and power. The lady of the house, a fierce journalist named Maahi Gupta, was at the center of a storm, her life suddenly entangled with the law in ways that neither she nor her household had anticipated.

Devraj watched from the kitchen as the house transformed into a battleground of legal minds and political power plays. Through the crackling of the hearth and the simmering of pots, he observed the tension that gripped Maahi, the fear that crept into the corners of her home, and the resolve that burned in her eyes. The story that unfolded was not just about one woman's fight against the system, but about the fragile nature of liberty itself, as seen through the eyes of a man who never expected to find himself at the crossroads of justice.

I remember the first day I set foot in the Gupta household. The year was 1977, and I, Devraj, had just been hired as the cook. The bustling Delos streets outside contrasted sharply with the calm within the gates of the Guptas' residence. The place was vast, with sprawling gardens and rooms that seemed to stretch endlessly. But it wasn't the grandeur of the house that struck me most—it was the atmosphere. Something heavy hung in the air, like the anticipation before a storm.

I was familiar with the name Maahi Gupta. Who wasn't? She was a renowned journalist, known for her fiery spirit and commitment to social causes. There were whispers among the other staff about some trouble she was in, something to do with her passport. But my job was to cook, not to pry into the affairs of the powerful.

My first few days were uneventful. I kept to the kitchen, preparing meals and avoiding the gaze of the visitors who came and went. But I could feel the tension growing. Maahiji seemed preoccupied, often pacing around the house, deep in thought. I overheard snippets of conversation—something about a passport being taken away and a court case that was causing quite a stir.

One evening, as I was preparing a simple dinner of dal and roti, Maahiji entered the kitchen. She rarely came in, leaving the kitchen matters to me and the maid, Kamala. But that night, she looked different — worn out, yet resolute.

"Devraj, could you make some tea?" she asked, her voice softer than usual.

I quickly obliged, noticing the weariness in her eyes as she sat down at the small kitchen table. I didn't dare ask what was wrong, but she must have seen the question in my eyes.

"They've taken my passport," she said, more to herself than to me. "No reason, no explanation. Just 'public interest,' they say."

I nodded, unsure of what to say. What did I know about passports or public interest? But even I, a lowly cook, did know injustice when I saw it, and there was something deeply wrong about this.

Days turned into weeks, and the house became a hive of activity. Lawyers, journalists, and activists streamed in and out, discussing the case in hushed tones. From the kitchen, I could hear their debates, their concerns about the future. The case had taken on a life of its own, becoming more than just about one woman's right to travel—it was now about the very essence of freedom.

I learned that Maahji was challenging the government's decision in the Supreme Court, arguing that the impounding of her passport violated her fundamental rights. It was not just about her personal liberty, but also about freedom of speech and expression, and the right to travel abroad. The government, on the other hand, cited vague notions of "public interest" to justify their actions.

The house was filled with legal books, documents, and people discussing complex constitutional principles—things far beyond my understanding. But the gravity of the situation was clear to me. Maahiji was not just fighting for herself; she was standing up against the arbitrary use of power by the state.

During this time, the kitchen became more than just a place for cooking. It was a sanctuary, a place where I could observe the unfolding drama without being noticed. Kamala and I would often discuss the case in whispers while preparing meals. She was more knowledgeable than I was about these things, having worked with other influential families before.

"It's not just about the passport, Devraj," she said one evening as we prepared dinner. "This case could change everything. If the court sides with her, it will mean that the government can't just do as it pleases with people's rights."

Her words stayed with me. I began to see the case in a new light, understanding that the outcome would affect not just Maahiji, but all of us. It was about our freedom, our rights as citizens. It was about whether the government could take away those rights without proper reason.

As the case progressed, the tension in the house grew. I could see the strain on Maahiji's face, the way she barely touched her food, the way she spent hours with her legal team, preparing for the hearings. The other staff and I tried to keep things running smoothly, but there was no escaping the sense of impending judgment.

Finally, the day of the verdict arrived. The house was eerily quiet, the usual bustle replaced by a tense silence. Maahiji had left early in the morning for the court, and we all waited anxiously for news.

When she returned, there was a different kind of silence—one filled with relief and triumph. She walked into the house, her face a mix of exhaustion and satisfaction. The verdict had been in her favor.

The Supreme Court had ruled that the impounding of her passport was unjust and violated her fundamental rights. The judgment was a landmark one, broadening the interpretation of the right to personal liberty under Article 21 of the Constitution. It was a victory not just for Maahiji, but for all citizens.

I later learned that the court had emphasized the need for laws to be fair, just, and reasonable, and that no person's rights could be taken away arbitrarily. The judgment also established the interconnection between Articles 14, 19, and 21, reinforcing the idea that personal liberty was sacrosanct.

For me, as a cook who had watched this drama unfold from the sidelines, it was a moment of immense pride. I had witnessed history being made, seen a woman stand up against the might of the state and win.

After the verdict, life at the Gupta household slowly returned to normal, but the impact of the case lingered. The house no longer buzzed with legal discussions, but there was a new sense of calm and purpose. Maahiji continued her work as a journalist and activist, but there was a renewed energy in her steps.

As for me, I continued to cook for the family, but with a deeper understanding of the world around me. I had seen how one person's courage could bring about change, how the fight for justice was not just the domain of the powerful, but something that affected all of us.

Years later, as I reflect on those days, I realize that the case was more than just a legal battle—it was a fight for the soul of our nation. It was about ensuring that our rights were protected, that the government could not overstep its bounds.

Maahiji's victory was a victory for all of us, a reminder that the power of the state must always be checked by the rights of the individual. And as I continue to prepare meals in the Gupta household, I carry with me the lessons of those days—the importance of standing up for what is right, of fighting for our freedoms, and of never underestimating the impact one person can have on the world.

In the quiet moments, as I chop vegetables or knead dough, I think of that time, of the resilience and determination I witnessed. And I am reminded that in the kitchen or in the courtroom, we all have our part to play in the pursuit of justice.

The actual case in the Indian judiciary system

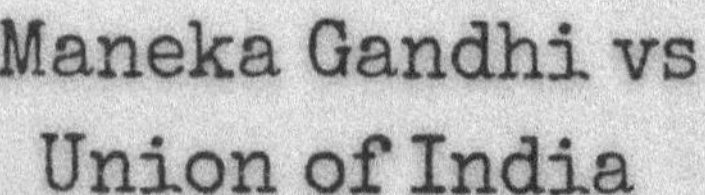

BACKGROUND INFORMATION

In 1977, Maneka Gandhi, a renowned journalist and social activist, was issued a passport by the Indian government. Shortly after, her passport was impounded under the Passport Act of 1967 without any specific reasons provided, citing "public interest.Maneka Gandhi challenged this decision, arguing that it violated her fundamental rights.

AIR 1978 SC 597

Maneka Gandhi

INCIDENT

Maneka Gandhi's legal team contended that the government's action infringed upon her right to personal liberty, freedom of speech and expression, and right to travel abroad as guaranteed under Articles 21 and 19 of the Indian Constitution. The case raised critical questions about the arbitrary exercise of state power and the extent of personal liberties.

IN THE COURTROOM

The case was heard by a seven-judge bench of the Supreme Court, which deliberated on the scope and interpretation of fundamental rights, especially Article 21 (Right to Life and Personal Liberty). The court also examined the procedural fairness and the reasonableness of the state's actions.

LANDMARK JUDGEMENT

The Supreme Court delivered a historic judgment, significantly broadening the interpretation of Article 21. It ruled that the right to personal liberty encompassed the right to travel abroad and that any restriction on this right must be just, fair, and reasonable. The court also emphasized the interconnection between Articles 14, 19, and 21, establishing that laws must be procedurally fair and not arbitrary.

IMPORTANCE

This case is a cornerstone in Indian constitutional law as it expanded the understanding of personal liberty and set a precedent for judicial scrutiny of state actions that infringe upon fundamental rights. The judgment strengthened the protection of individual freedoms against arbitrary state actions and underscored the importance of due process.

Contact Relatives 

Brief Chief 

Crime Scene Visit

Notes

Notes

Notes